Parenting Young Toddlers

The Simplified Childrens Book with Perfect Ways

of Caring for Your Baby and Raising a Child

Regina Williams

Table of Contents

PARENTING YOUNG TODDLERS 1

PREFACE 4

INTRODUCTION 6

CHAPTER 1 10
  How to improve a Child Behavior 10

CHAPTER 2 16
  How to Enjoy Parenting Your Child 16
    Positive way to Raise a Child 17
    What to Check Before You Right-Off Children 19
    Parenting without Yelling 22

CHAPTER 3 25
  Methods for Raising a Child 25

CHAPTER 4 30
  The Twenty Commandments of Toddler Self-Discipline 30

CHAPTER 5 37
  How to Self-Discipline a Young Child? 29 Child Self-Discipline Techniques that Work 37

Copyright © 2020 by Regina Williams

All rights reserved. No part of this publication may be reproduced, distributed, or transmitted in any form or by any means, including photocopying, recording, or other electronic or mechanical methods, without the prior written permission of the publisher, except in the case of brief quotations embodied in critical reviews and certain other non-commercial uses permitted by copyright law.

ISBN: 978-1-63750-247-1

Preface

Do you know that discovering and understanding how to flow perfectly with your toddlers and how to assist the youngster walk while pressing the wheel during playtime is important in parenting?

This book is centered on how to simply help parents understand what is expected of them while parenting toddlers which begins with;

- ✓ understanding how to improve a child behaviour,
- ✓ how to positively raise a child,
- ✓ how to enjoy parenting,
- ✓ methods of raising a child,
- ✓ how to self-discipline a young child,

…and many more in a simplified form.

This book is concise and easy to read, understand and the knowledge therein are applicable within 30mins of reading to completion.

There is undoubtedly an array of what might look like *'normal'* development. Nevertheless, relating to experts will make one understand that particular milestones need to be attained by specific age groups and phases in every area of their lives.

This book will help several parents achieve proper parenting of their toddlers in a more simplified and concise approach.

Small children are subconsciously known for their childish display and other behavioral issues. To encourage hearing and listening to you, follow proper parenting ideas explained in this book.

Introduction

Discovering and understanding how to flow perfectly with your kids and how to assist the youngster walk while pressing the wheel during playtime.

The progressive pattern of a child's growth is divided into lots of related areas, and there are reasonable opinions as to what these areas consist of:

- **Physical development:** This includes the child's physical growth (increase in size).

- **Primary motion skills:** The controls of huge muscles which usually allow the child to stroll, operate, jump, and rise.

- **Excellent motion skills:** the capability to control small muscle tissue, allowing the child to give food to themselves, pull, and manipulate items.

- **Vision:** the capability to see closely and translate what is noticed.

- **Hearing and speech:** the capability to hear, get

information, and pay attention (interpret), and also the ability to understand and find out about vocabulary and utilize it to connect effectively.

- **Sociable:** the capability to connect to the globe through others.

Although it is better to use graph to define intervals of advancement, additionally, it is essential to notice that advancement exists continuously.

There is undoubtedly an array of what might look like *'normal'* development. Nevertheless, relating to experts will make one understand that particular milestones need to be attained by specific age groups and phases in every area of their lives.

Twelve months aged

In twelve months old, the average child should be able to see the following abilities:

- Physical and motion skills.
- An average one-year-old toddler's body ratios.

- Triple the delivery weight.
- Grow to an elevation of 50 per cent over delivery length.
- Possess a mind circumference to add up to that of the chest.
- I have got some 1 - 8 teeth.
- Draw to stand.
- Walk with help or alone.
- Sit back without help.
- Bang two blocks with each other.
- Flip through the pages of a book by flicking many pages at the same time.
- Possess a pincer grasp.
- Rest 8-10 hours a night time and consider one or two naps.
- Sensory and cognitive advancement.

- Understanding how to eat independently.

- It comes after an accessible shifting object.

- Responds to his/her name.

- Understands several words.

- Can easily say mom, papa, with least a couple of other terms.

- Understands basic commands.

- Attempts to replicate pet noises.

- Connects titles with items.

- Understands that items exist, even though they aren't seen.

Chapter 1

How to improve a Child Behavior

Small children are subconsciously known for their childish display and other behavioral issues. To encourage hearing and assistance, follow proper parenting ideas.

Getting acquainted with children could make life frustrating. As much as we intend to be fair enough, children can not move as quickly as we want them to, as they will always want to communicate their needs, which has no limit (they have issues with bargaining and dissatisfaction). This, most times, may lead to tantrums and misbehaviors.

Nevertheless, you may train your child to act well by giving crystal clear guidelines and an amount of routine with love. Carefully examine these useful tips.

- *Display your feelings*

Ensure that the love you show to your son or daughter out-numbers any punishments. Hugs, kisses, and good-nature re-assures your son or daughter of how much you appreciate them; the same way compliments and attention can also motivate your child.

- ***Prioritize guidelines***

Instead of overloading your son or daughter with rules and principles from your point of view, which can get him/her angry, prioritize the ones aimed toward health and safety first and steadily add tips as time goes by. Help your child adhere to the guidelines by simply child-proofing your house and removing some lure.

- ***Prevent tantrums***

It's regular for a child to have temper tantrums and to lessen the rate of recurrence, period or strength of your son or daughter's tantrums, you should;

<u>Understand your son or daughter's limitations</u> – Precisely, your son or daughter may misbehave if he/she does not understand what you are requesting.

Find out how to check and adjust your rules and principles; rather than saying, *"Stop striking"* you can offer recommendations and steps to do something else instead

Take 'no' as a sign of progress - Don't overreact whenever your young child says no, alternatively you could make an effort, compelling them to do it again. You could also make an effort to make the task fun by playing any game. Your son or daughter could be more likely to do what you would like if you make a task fun.

Pick your fights - If you say only no to everything, your son or daughter will probably get discouraged. Carefully observe occasions when it's okay to say yes.

Offer options, when feasible - Encourage your son or daughter's independence by merely allowing her/him pick out a set of pajamas or a bedtime tale.

Prevent situations that may trigger disappointment or tantrums - For instance, avoid giving your son or daughter play toys that are too advanced for her or him. Avoid lengthy outings where your child must sit down even if he/she can or cannot play. Also, know that kids will take action out when they're exhausted, hungry, ill, or within an unfamiliar environment.

Adhere to the routine - Maintain a day to day routine, which means that your kid will know very well what to expect.

Motivate communication - Help remind your son or daughter to use terms expressing his/her emotions. If your son or daughter isn't very outspoken, consider teaching her or him baby sign language to avoid disappointment.

Enforce effects - Despite your very best efforts, sooner or later, your child can break the guidelines. Ignore small shows of anger, for instance, "if a child strike, kicks or screams pertaining for a long period,"; carefully help the child with whatever problem it is. Consider using these child-rearing tips to motivate your son or daughter to cooperate.

Organic consequences – Allow your son or daughter to see the result of his/her actions, so long as they're risk-free. For instance, if your son or daughter throws and breaks a toy, he/she won't possess the gadget again, to avoid repetition of damage.

Reasonable consequences – Make sure everything your child needs for him/her activities is well provided and make him/her know that if he/she does not grab the play toys, you would have to put the toys aside for the rest of the day. Help your son or daughter with the various activities, if required. If your son or daughter does not cooperate, make him/her know the consequence.

Withholding liberties - If your son or daughter misbehave, ensure that you keep away within his/her reach that particular thing that makes him/her act like that, e.g., a favorite toy or something which is related to his/her misbehavior.

Timeout - Whenever your child acts up, go down to his/her level, briefly and calmly clarify why the behavior is undesirable. If the indigent behavior proceeds, guide your son or daughter to a specified timeout place, preferably a silent area without interruptions. Enforce the timeout till your son or daughter is relaxed and may pay attention to you. Afterward, assure your son or daughter of the love and guide you have for him/her.

Whatever consequences you select, be constant - Ensure that every single adult who also cares about your son or daughter observes these same guidelines and discipline recommendations.

Also, be cautious about criticizing your son or daughter's behavior. Spanking, slapping, and shouting at a kid should never be suitable.

Set an example - children understand how to do something only by seeing what their parents also do. The ultimate way to show your son or daughter how to act is to create an optimistic example for her or him to follow.

Chapter 2
How to Enjoy Parenting Your Child

You have survived the sleepless evenings and never-ending feeding cycles of the baby stage, you have had a while to cuddle cute baby cheeks and have a look at every new developing milestone, and before you know it, that phase of life is over.

Parenting small children is similar to getting into a new globe; as kids are acquainted in doing things like:

They can speak - however, the common term they use is definitely *"no."*

They can walk - however they can also try to escape from you in parking lots.

They could be impartial – this happens most times when they are getting old, within the age of 2-4.

Here are some tips to ensure that children and pre-schoolers give a measure of respect to their parents. Keeping the partnership with your son or daughter is substantial, robust, and healthful and even learns how to take pleasure from these years of training.

Positive way to Raise a Child

How to favorably mother or father your child

If you're like the majority of parents, you would like to go directly into discipline because not going straight into the discipline stage will help the toddler build up the sense of self-discipline; but when you skip this part, parenting them is likely to be a headache than a pleasure.

You're most likely heading to end up in a never-ending power challenge, intense, weird behavior, and legendary meltdowns.

Positive parenting requires a different approach. This ideology helps us relax and connect well with our children (even when they are misbehaving), it will also help them through emotional issues and teach them lessons in ways that are most reliable.

This form of parenting helps to improve the child's behavior, which means whenever your kid starts acting up, you will have to put age group, developing stage, and brain maturity into consideration. You may end up realizing that your son or daughter is confused about a particular situation and only need rest.

Every point made are entirely meaningful solutions and strategies that work, solutions that make you feel relaxed and in charge.

Ok, Let's speak about how exactly parents can discipline small children. But first, let us clarify between *"self-discipline" and "consequence."*

"Punishment" is targeted on creating a penalty that causes agonizing to instruct your son or daughter. *"Self-discipline,"* on the other hand, seeks to steer your child, assisting them to get a much better method to control the problem in the foreseeable future instead of punishing.

It may appear just like a small selection of words; however, it can make an enormous difference in just how you react to your son or daughter. The pattern of training shouldn't be centered on insults (or in case you were raised with parents who used punishment), you might use that as a yardstick and start seeing your son or daughter as "bad" or "misbehaving" or "bratty." You might believe that they have to "get away with their bad behavior," or by punishing them, they will learn their lessons." Regrettably, this does not create a stable romantic relationship, and you will likely dislike parenting through the child years.

Nevertheless, if you observe your son or daughter, after being punished, you might feel compassionate. You'd have to look for techniques to use on them, support them as they struggle, or react with sympathy.

This might not be the "discipline" you're acquainted with; however, it can be a fantastic way to create your child's psychological intelligence, enhance their problem-solving abilities, grow sympathy for others, and it maintains your romantic relationship strong and healthy.

What to Check Before You Right-Off Children

Child Meltdowns and Tantrums

Support your son or daughter's independence and problem resolving using these five actions before you correct or suggest a much better solution.

No-one can throw a tantrum much better than a young child. It's a full-body encounter that often leaves parents sense overwhelmed, surprised, and ashamed.

Thankfully, tantrums are standard through the toddler and preschool years. It's hard to understand everything about the toddler at ones.

Using positive child-rearing and sincere discipline, it is possible to decrease the number of tantrums and the strength of the meltdowns your son or daughter encounters throughout the day.

Reading More as Regards Supporting Your Child, Managing Tantrums.

A parent needs to read books as regards;

- How to Manage Young child bad temper
- How to Help Your bad temper Kid relax

Common Concerns intended for Parents of Toddlers

Sick and tired of wanting your son or daughter in control, and you don't have much power to hold them back? Use these assured pointers to help you exhibit an experienced parenting.

The challenge parents face about a child's growth is not just self-discipline; there are also some other challenges that pop-up subconsciously. Thankfully, the majority of problems aren't unique. A few appear like a norm, every child must try as they grow and mature.

Utilize this list to assist yourself react when these issues arrive, also have it at the back of your mind that each child differs. You might be an expert with your son or daughter, but anytime you see something unusual or concerning, don't hesitate to speak to the doctor or a mental wellness provider.

Assisting Your Son or Daughter through Separation Stress

Are you crazy early morning with children?

Here's a way to get out the entranceway on time; My Child will not Stop Speaking! How you can mother or father small children and young children: sibling competition

- Parenting a toddler is severe enough, yet put in a couple of other children in the blend, and suddenly, you have a couple of new challenges at hand.

- Instead of expecting your baby to control these interpersonal skills easily, provide them with the support they want as they figure out how to share playthings, make changes, and argue without harming another kid.

Parenting without Yelling

These pointers and approaches for parenting children are excellent theoretically; however, they can quickly appear impossible if you don't know how to manage your anger.

You do not want to yell; however, you are trying to put up your best act so you won't hurt the kids, and this act leaves you somewhat in the aftermath of the situation.

Several factors will require parents shouting - feeling uncontrollable, being unsure of how to react, fretting about how many other people believe, panicking that you're ruining your child…etc.

Instead of remaining trapped, you will try as much as possible to get your mind off the yelling. Make new strategies, which will help give you a lot of persistence, and help you remain optimistic.

When you start yelling at your children, it might be quite tricky to stop or to shift from an unaggressive mother or father to a confident mother or father.

There are times your son or daughter will expect you to intensify, but it shouldn't be every time

Mother or Father Coaching

Raising a small children and pre-schoolers may be considered a concern, but it may also be isolating and complicated. An instant Google search can provide you 1 million different answers, as well as your friends' raising a child style, might not exactly match how you need to parent.

You don't have to do the whole parenting by yourself; there is also support, and support is obtainable. Getting knowledge on how to Mother or father a child online is usually safe, sound, and non-judgmental as you find the training pattern, excellent for you as well as your kid.

Raising a child is similar to entering a new world.

- They can talk -- they state the sexiest, most unpredicted things.

- They can walk -- making a casino game of run after or ring-around-the-rosy much more fun!

- They could become independent -- it is incredible watching them develop and find out.

Chapter 3
Methods for Raising a Child

- *Tantrums are a standard part of the advancement*

Whenever a child has a crisis, they may be interacting around and also releasing their particular emotions. This is one-way small children exhibit overwhelm, dread, aggravation, and disappointment.

- *Impacting is undoubtedly the main element of cooperation.*

It is natural actually to want to regulate something when it seems uncontrollable. Nevertheless, we really can't control some other things. When we make an effort to control a child, this usually leads to contention in power. We can control our very own behavior and try as much as possible to let the child imitate us. Partnering with your child and working together as a team most time has a positive effect through connection and co-operation. Conversely, control creates a routine of the level of resistance.

- *Concentrate on the positivity*

Did you ever hear that *"Everything you concentrate on develops?"* This perspective provides a significant effect on thoughts, emotions, and feelings. Practice this by informing your son or daughter what exactly they are successful at, also take out time to celebrate what is working well for them. Getting focus on these advantages reinforces the child and leaves everyone's senses more strengthened.

- *Connection is key*

Small children can be indie in an instant, and yet they will remain exceptionally emotionally reliant on us. That is why relationship plays an essential function in toddlerhood. Linking with your son or daughter within a challenging instant helps take them back to their particular psychological balance and raises their connection. When there is a good connection, a small child tends to learn, develop, and flourish.

- *Pay attention to be paid attention to*

It's a pure normal for a human to notice and feel noticed. The fact that the parents are already old and have vast knowledge about life doesn't imply that we ought to look down on a toddler's emotions, feelings, and thoughts. The quickest way to obtain a child to avoid hearing you is to avoid hearing all of them.

- *Almost all emotions and feelings are Alright but not all actions*

As humans, we are programmed to see a full spectral range of emotions. Allowing your son or daughter understand that emotions and feelings okay help change their mindset, but validating emotions does not mean you need to condone some of their particular behaviors. Rather than shutting straight down their emotions and feelings, help your child to sort them out. Out of this place, you can help them figure out how to communicate their feelings and emotions with proper behaviour.

- *Get interested in behaviour*

Attention is one of the very most effective tools we have in child-rearing. Getting engaged in your toddler's behaviour enables you to learn all of them on a much deeper level and prevents you from becoming the assets and court. This attention creates connection and gives you time to respond rather than reacting when you are feeling disappointed.

- *Concentrate on what is causing the behaviour, not the behavior itself*

Emotions, feelings, and needs power your toddler's behaviour. That is why the simplest way to improve behavior isn't merely by concentrating on the behavior itself. It is by focusing on the main from the action of the real cause. Dealing with their emotions, feelings, and needs changes behaviour.

- *Action is the most crucial work*

The main job a toddler offers is to try out. Making time for unstructured, creative enjoyment provides your child a wholesome feeling of autonomy and control as they find out and grasp new abilities.

- *Help them meet up with expectations*

Small children have spent just a little while on earth and still need more time to learn so many things about how to get acquainted with this globe. Sometimes they may be developmentally struggling, and they are going to inform you about their behaviour.

The simplest way you can help them isn't by insults and abuse but by teaching them the abilities they have to understand to meet up with the expectation in the foreseeable future.

I request you to take a breath, and allow it away gradually, provide yourself an enormous hug. You awaken every day and do the very best you can.

Change doesn't happen overnight -- it takes a while, practice, and support. Every day serves as an opportunity and a foundation to prepare for what comes next.

If a parent makes any mistake, such a parent should not dwell so much on the error. Most parents do make mistakes. Such a mistake should be seen as an opportunity to learn. Every single minute can be an invitation to start once again.

Chapter 4

The Twenty Commandments of Toddler Self-Discipline

It's not good to let your son or daughter get too comfortable with rules and implications just because of the connection and good relationship.

Children that are not necessarily given birth to sociable abilities often have the individual character of *survival-of-the-fittest mindset*. That is why you should train your child how to do some things and do them appropriately and securely.

The seed products of self-discipline will bloom later, and you will be very impressed by the fruits of your labour. Listed below are the commandments you ought to invest in:

1. **Anticipate tight places** - Certain circumstances and occasions of your day tend to result in bad behaviour. There is a fundamental belief that a transition from one activity to another gives your

son or daughter a heads-up, so he is more ready for upgrades.

2. **Choose your fights** - If you state "no" twenty times per day, the word "no" will eventually lose its value. Prioritize actions into massive, medium, and the ones too minor to work with.

3. **Make use of a prevent protection** - Help to make your home kid-friendly, and also have affordable expectations. If you clear your Swarovski amazingly collection away from the finish desk, your son or daughter will not be enticed to fling it all at its set. If you are taking your loved ones out to supper, go early, and that means you refuse to have to hold back for a desk.

4. **Make your claims short and sweet** - Speak in short phrases, this kind of as "No striking. That is a lot more effective than…" "Chaz, you understand it isn't good going to your dog." You will lose Chaz immediately after inches, you know.

5. **Distract and refocus** – for instance, if your son or daughter unrolls the whole toilet-paper move for the 10th period today, smoothly remove her from the toilet and close the entranceway.

6. **Introduce effects** - Your son or daughter ought to learn the organic results of his behaviour. For instance, if he fully insists upon selecting his pajamas (which requires a long time), after that, he's also choosing never to read books before bed. *Cause: Continuous picking of pajamas Impact*: Virtually no time to read. The next time, he might select his pajamas quicker or allow you to choose them away.

7. **No longer back off to prevent discord** - If you decide that your son or daughter doesn't have the cereal that she noticed on TV, adhere to your weapons. Later, you will be happy you do.

8. **Anticipate offers for interest** - Yes, your little angel will work up whenever your attention is usually diverted, making supper or speaking on the

phone. That is why it's necessary to provide several entertainments (a favourite gadget or an instant treat).

9. **Concentrate on the behaviour, not the kid** – you should say particular actions are wrong, but by no means should you inform your son or daughter that he/she is wrong.

10. **Give your son or daughter choices** - This can make her feel like she has a say. Be sure you avoid offering him/her too many options.

11. **Have a tender yell** – you can yell, but change your tone of voice. It most times amounts to nothing when you scream at the top of your voice; however, the firmness of your voice passes the information across.

12. **Catch your son or daughter being good** - If you praise your son or daughter when this individual behaves well, he'll get it done more regularly -- and he could be less inclined to act merely to get the attention. Positive encouragement is usually fertilizer for the super-ego.

13. **Take action instantly** – don't wait for your child to understand somethings usually, don't think your child can self-discipline him/herself always.

14. **Be considered a great role model** - If you are quiet under high pressure, your son or daughter will need the cue. And if you have a temper fit if you are annoyed, except that he will do the same. He is watching you, always watching.

15. **Do not treat your son or daughter as though she has grown-up** - The lady does not want to listen to a spiel from you -- and will not be in a position to understand it. Next time she includes her spaghetti, don't break right into the "you can't toss your meal." Steadily evict her from your kitchen for the night time.

16. **Make use of time-outs even as of this age group.** Call it up the kinky seat or whatever you prefer, but consider your son or daughter from playing and do not focus on him for just one minute for every 12 months old. Starving him of attention is

the simplest way to get your message throughout. Realistically, children under two won't sit down in a corner or on the seat, and it's outstanding to allow them to be on to the floor kicking and screaming. Just make sure the time-out location can be a secure one. Reserve time-outs for especially inappropriate behaviours if your son or daughter attacks his pal's arm, such as and use a time-out each time the offense happens.

17. **Can not negotiate with your son or daughter or make guarantees.** This is not Capitol Hill. Stay away from stating anything at all like, inches If you act, I'll purchase you that doll you want. Inch Normally, you will produce a 3-year-old whose excellent behavior will usually feature a price.

18. **Change your strategies as time passes.** What worked well superbly whenever your child was 15 weeks probably isn't very heading to work when he's two. He'll have got read your playbooks and viewed the films.

19. **Don't spank.** Although you might be tempted sometimes, understand that you will be the parent. Don't

vacate resort to performing just like a kid. You will find a lot more effective means of getting the message across. Fresh your son or daughter about striking or kicking you, for example, only shows him that it is alright to make use of pressure. Finally, if your child is pressing your control keys for the umpteenth period, and you also believe you're going to lose this, make an effort to have a step back again. You'll get a much better notion of which usually manipulative manners your son or daughter is generally using, and you will get a brand new perspective about how to improve your approach.

20. Remind your son or daughter that you like her. It certainly is good to get rid of a self-discipline conversation with an optimistic comment. This displays your son or daughter that you have been prepared to move ahead rather than place the issue. Also, it reinforces the reason why most likely setting limitations since you like her.

Chapter 5

How to Self-Discipline a Young Child? 29 Child Self-Discipline Techniques that Work

Discouraged with your children's antics? Disciplining small children could be difficult. Below are a few discipline methods that genuinely work.

My 2½-year-old child, Zoe, is undoubtedly gaining her shoes. The girl happily displays her handiwork. "Nice job, Zoe, " I say. "I want to change them. " I draw on the Velcro strap. Zoe jerks her foot aside and glares at me: "Shoes stay, Mommy. " I continue. "Bad Mommy. No. " Tears fall as the girl scoots from me. We picked and chose her up and set her in the truck, mismatched shoes or boots, and everything. Even as we mind toward the recreation area, I question: MUST I possess insisted? MUST I did something about the "Bad Mommy" comment? MUST I have terminated our trip?

Works out, I walked into a typical young child scenario just about guaranteed to get rid of incompatible. Zoe was attempting to say her new-found self-reliance, displaying me personally her new skill. We not just reduced her achievement, I began undoing her effort without detailing, at her level, so why the shoes would have to be switched. The lady does what small children carry out when they get frustrated: Eyelash out and cry.

"Parents need to comprehend that kids are designed to learn and test. And some of this behaviour parents may see misbehaviour. They will want to end up being self-employed; however, they don't have the abilities and get frustrated, " says Linda Gilbert, supervisor of teaching, youngsters, and family advancement at the YMCA of Higher Toronto. The girl with concentration on this age group must be on controlling behaviour, not self-discipline as a result.

Denise Marshall, an early on child years educator at the University or college of Northern Uk Columbia Daycare Culture in Prince George, BC, wants: " What's 'bad' behavior anyway? A child's description and a parent's look at tend to be completely different: You inform your child to place a gadget away. This individual doesn't. You view it seeing that defiance. This individual does not want to avoid playing. "

All the industry experts agree that children will certainly "misbehave" when our anticipations are past their capabilities. For instance, it isn't convenient to anticipate a child to check out a string of instructions, or even to remember a guideline after being told only one time.

" You must keep vocabulary basic. A lot is occurring in their minds. It's essential to do it again yourself; otherwise, it'll get overlooked."

To keep objectives realistic, it is beneficial to be familiar with developmental elements that impact toddler behavior:

- *Social abilities*

At 1.5 years, toddlers are beginning to end up being thinking about getting together with other children, using all of them rather than hand in hand. But the guidelines of sociable play aren't instinctive -- kids have to be trained regarding taking converts and getting mild. Intense behavior, such mainly because biting, is usually normal, says Gail Szautner, chairperson from the Saskatchewan Early Child years Association and professional director of Children's Choice Child Advancement Programs in Prince Albert, Sask. "It's developmental. It is the way they respond."

Also healthy may be the reluctance to talk about it. "Developmentally, these are not looking forward to coping with only one pickup truck or regularly taking transforms.

- ***Self-control***

Most of the defiance that people attribute toddler behavior is due to their particular limited capability to regulate their specific impulses. Your girl might know that chucking food from the high seat is a no-no, yet try because she may, the desire to see her mac and cheese move splat on to the floor can be overpowering.

Alternatively, whenever a toddler's urges and wishes are discouraged, the reaction could be intense. (And there is undoubtedly a lot of stress within a toddler's globe: from the noodle that will not stick to the spoon towards the grown-up who doesn't know very well what she's attempting to state.) It's very hard on her behalf to rein in her anger and resist the desire to hit, toss or have a tantrum.

- *Psychological regulation*

Kids have trouble understanding their particular feelings, aside from controlling all of them. Plus, they do not have the perspective or encounter to understand the fact that deep unhappiness they experience more than a damaged cookie will certainly soon complete. "Small children need help to identify and deal using their emotions, Together with your reassuring hugs, it could be useful to expose self-soothing techniques, such as embracing a popular plaything, sipping water or inhaling and exhaling deeply.

- *Sympathy*

" Small children have a budding knowing of others, yet are self-centered, " says Delorey-McGowan. It is because of this that they have a problem with empathy -- they do not recognize that others respond adversely to discomfort or disappointment. This also explains as to why a child may react inappropriately to some other child's feelings, like laughing whenever a playmate pinches, he submits the toy upper body.

- **Comprehension**

How can a kid stick to instructions if he does understand no benefits are being asked of him? Vocabulary and attention abilities are just growing in toddlerhood, so it is essential never to overestimate what kids may comprehend-that can only lead to annoyance on both sides. Says Marshall: "Children could know very well what parents are requesting, but it is hard to check out directions just how we wish these to. Adults require to steer all of them."

Even if your son or daughter can know very well what you're stating, he might not be attending. "I do not see any child exactly who listens regularly. You must get on their level and make the vision get in touch with.

- ***What works***

Just how exactly, is it possible to guide your child's conduct? Just like your son or daughter is tinkering with her behaviour, you'll need to test out your self-discipline methods, depending on her age, character as well as your beliefs. Specialists share their particular favourite strategies:

1. Prevent

"Always believe forward: 'How may I get this an effective day time?'" says Gilbert. This implies setting up the surroundings to market excellent behavior. If your son or daughter is actually into dressing herself, be sure you have plenty of trousers with flexible waists and shirts that are easy to put up to lessen aggravation. And invite more time to get dressed up in the morning.

With regards to playdates, strategize forward to reduce conflict. Suggests ensuring there are enough toys to talk about (duplicates if required) and several actions to lessen the boredom.

A kid who's starving, thirsty, exhausted or hurried is much more likely to misbehave, so forgoing a treat or planning for a playdate during nap period is a surefire trip on the Crisis Express.

2. Offer choices

Because small children are tinkering with self-reliance, it is essential to provide them secure, reasonable probabilities to say this: " Would you like your juice in glass or the green cup? " " Would you like to go directly to the recreation area in your lorry or the baby stroller? " Provides Delorey-McGowan, "Toddlers want to make options. If you state no, they need it much more. "

3. Supervise

It all might not appear, such as a self-discipline tool; nevertheless, you can't help your son or daughter find out appropriate actions if you are not there to teach him. This doesn't mean stepping directly into solve every single problem but instead guiding him about how to behave: " I understand you wish to decrease the slide, yet Ruby is definitely before you. She'll move, and you'll be able to go." As well as the more you view, the higher you will have the ability to inform what circumstances set him off and ways to help.

4. Arranged targets and consequences

Kids can't adhere to the guidelines if indeed they don't know very well what they are. Make specific instructions and guidelines are obvious and essential, says Szautner. "Establish eye-to-eye contact and be sure she's nodding when you speak to her."

Marshall gives that directions apply "I" charm to small children who wish to make sure you: "I'm frightened you will fall from the seat. Please sit back."

And become clear in what may happen if guidelines aren't followed: "We pull just in writing. In case you attract up for grabs again, all of us must place the crayons aside."

5. *Show and tell*

Small children are apparent, says Szautner, even though terms are essential, therefore is modeling the behavior you need. Consider change happening by way of example. You could attempt stating: "It's your switch to place the cent in the money box, today it's my convert, at this point it's your change …"

6. *Compliment*

As single-minded as small children are, they will still need to make sure you are enhancing your them, when he approaches the table the very first time you inquire not just show him what excellent behavior it is usually, it also reinforces your relationship. "Children require a lot of attention; that is our work as parents. Be cautious about providing a focus on proper behavior, " says Szautner.

7. *Refocus*

"If you visit a fit building, distract them with something they prefer to do, " suggests Szautner. In case your 2½-

year-old is disappointed that her old sibling won't talk about her new doll, state, "Let's get your peel off stickers at your kitchen desk. " And as of this age group, children like to help; keep these things assist you to put the condiments up for grabs or place the clean towels aside.

Redirection may also "unstick" your child from a no-no the lady can't log off her brain. If she's attracted just like a magnet to Grandma's audio system, get her involved with a new activity.

Along with redirection, identifying a child's feelings might be helpful: "It appears like you're upset that most took your vehicle. Would you like to go directly to the sofa beside me and relax? "

8. Remove

Delorey-McGowan suggests creating an appropriate, silent place exactly where your son or daughter can be with you when he has lost control. It is not a consequence, but instead a spot to relax -- the sofa, a step within the stairs or an area for the carpet which includes cushy cushions.

9. Consider what you do

Even though it appears to seem sensible to speak to a kid after an incident of misbehaviour, that is pointless with toddlers, says Gail Szautner, executive director of Children's Choice Kid Development Applications in Knight in shining armor Albert, Sask. " So far as they are worried, it's carried out. Getting up again will not accomplish anything at all. They aren't developmentally presently there yet. "

10. Say sorry

You can not make a kid feel bad. Which strategy sends the message that are striking, for instance, it's fine as long as the girl apologizes after.

11. "No, no, simply no, no…. "

It's more beneficial to show - and possess - kids how to proceed instead of what never to do. Rather than "No shouting, " try "Please make use of a peaceful tone of voice " -- and state it silently. You will find situations in which a company simply no (in conjunction with swift action) is necessary. But conserve no meant for when you genuinely need it.

12. " Okay, OK, you could have the right path."

Sometimes, in spite of our perfect attempts, small children pitch a fit or won't end up being swayed. Become sympathetic, yet don't give in. Your son or daughter must discover that you mean whatever you say, and they are strong enough to stand, even when confronted with toddler rage.

13. " I do this my way."

Kate, a single, and her mother are experiencing fun filling up containers with water and dumping all of them into the shower. Then Kate pours water onto the ground. "Water remains in the bathtub, Kate. " Kate fills the box, discusses Mother and dumps water on to the floor once again. Now what?

14. Established clear goals

Ensure that your guidelines are apparent, and she hears you: " If you toss water from the tub once again, I'll take those glass aside." Old toddlers might react by asking you why and you can reply thus: " pouring water on to the floor is usually dangerous. It could make all of us fall. "

15. Refocus

Make an effort to make the filling of water in the tub more exciting -- sing a popular song jointly or bring in a different toy. "Your duckies require water to go swimming in the tub. "

16. Provide options

" Would you like to put water on your hands or on your legs? "

17. Remove

If dropping water continues, remove her from the tub and clarify why: "You're not hearing; therefore, you're likely to have to turn out. "

18. Consequences

I have got her to assist you to tidy up water showing the results of her activities: " Water needs to be mopped mainly because someone can slide. "

19. "Mine, mine, mine."

James, two, and Mike, 2½, are performing in Sam's home. James accumulates the green vehicle; Mike lunges for this: "My pickup truck! " Wayne resists.

20. Prevent

Having loads of duplicates might avoid this example altogether, yet sometimes nothing at all will do; however, the very vehicle that's in the various other child's hands.

21. Arranged anticipations and consequences

Make the guidelines visible: "These toys and games are intended for posting. We can play with all of them as long as we all may make changes. "

22. Supervise

Since toddlers require plenty of training in public abilities, it's crucial to carefully watch over kids who also are playing together.

www.ingramcontent.com/pod-product-compliance
Lightning Source LLC
Chambersburg PA
CBHW071038080526
44587CB00015B/2669